Ebb & Flow

A Guide to Help You Recover from a Broken Heart &
Broken Relationships

Dr. Tracey R. Brown

TRBZ Enterprises
DALLAS, TEXAS

TRBZ Enterprises
P.O. Box 75138-1456
Duncanville, Texas 75138
www.drtraceybrown.com

Publisher's Note: Locales and public names are sometimes used for atmospheric purposes. Scripture references are taken from the Holy Bible.
Printed in the United States of America
First Printing, 2015

Editors: Tonya Brown, Vaughn Price
Cover Design: El Creative, Inc.
Photography: El Creative, Inc.
Editing/Project Consultant: Gwen Cash/GDCash, LLC

Ordering Information:
Quantity sales. Special discounts are available on quantity purchases by corporations, associations, and others. For details, contact the "Special Sales Department" at the address above.

Ebb & Flow/ Tracey Brown.
ISBN 978-0-9912209-2-2

DEDICATION

This book is dedicated to my beautiful family—Zachary, Barbara, Jessie, Lorenzo, Gwen, Rhonda, and Tonya. Thank you for being an anchor in the middle of my storm!

Table of Contents

Introduction 1

It's Okay to Not Be Okay 5

Broken Pieces..............11

God & Time 17

Make Good Decisions 23

Get Rid of PQRs..............29

Love Anyway 35

Forgive Yourself 43

Be Comfortable in Your Own Skin..............47

The Quiet in the Storm 53

Defeat the Giant Within..............61

Synchronize Your Heart, Mind, Body, & Soul 69

Take Time to Heal 75

Find Your Rhythm 81

Present in the Moment..............87

Appreciate the Wait..............91

Push Forward 97

Love Yourself..............103

(Un)Solved Mysteries..............109

Faith, Fidelity, & Finesse 117

Uniquely You!..............123

Find Your Reason to Live! 129

My Prayer for You… 135

ABOUT THE AUTHOR 137

Introduction

I n the spring of 2014, I released my first book entitled, SINGLE MOM, PHD. My goal was to share the challenges I faced in my journey as a single mom and the deep emotional pain I experienced as I walked through single motherhood alone. The anxiety I felt was enormous, and the pain of it left me broken and wounded on the inside. The tumultuous relationship I had with my co-parent made it all the more unbearable as I felt lost wondering what to do with the challenges in front of me.

Our relationship had its ups and downs and posed several problems to which neither of us had the answers. We were both wounded and unable to navigate our way through the storms that raged between us and the hurt that resided within us. We were broken and in need of someone to help us put the pieces of our hearts back together again.

Personally, I knew that if I was going to survive, I would need an anchor to hold me steady as I navigated my way through one of the most difficult times of my life. I knew that if I was going to make it through, my soul would need to heal and my heart would need to find rest from the raging storms within.

The pain of my experiences as a single mom not only taught me valuable lessons in life, but has become the driving force behind my passion for writing *Ebb & Flow*.

To "ebb" is to decline, retreat, or move away from something. This term is often used to describe the behavior of the ocean tide as it recedes, or moves away from the land out to the sea. This concept of "ebbing" is an analogy used to describe the decline we experience in our lives when we feel we are at our wit's end and unable to deal with the deep emotional pain that comes from the loss of something or someone we hold near and dear to our heart.

To "flow", on the other hand, is to move toward something in a steady stream. Related to the ocean, the waters move toward the land, steadily and continuously, creating a floodgate that brings massive waves ashore. Applied to our own life, flow occurs when our understanding is enlightened and the floodgates fill our heart with love, joy, peace and the wealth of blessings that are in store for us to receive.

Thus, the phrase "ebb and flow" in this guide will refer to the continuous, rhythmic pattern of ups and downs and the decisions we make about these fluctuations that determine our course of action in life and relationships.

It is often said that it takes 21 days to change a behavior and form new habits. It is for this reason that I have written *Ebb & Flow*. This meditational guide provides 21 days of insights that offer you a fresh perspective of life and help you confront some of the negative circumstances you might be experiencing in your relationships.

I have also included "Daily Affirmations" at the beginning of each day's meditation that are small nuggets of wisdom to consider throughout your day. I believe these affirmations will help you fight against negative thoughts that come to mind as you work through the pain you might be experiencing from a broken heart and broken relationships.

I invite you to use the "Reflections and Insights" section to journal how you feel about the topic for each day and note ways you can develop and grow in various areas of your life. Jotting your thoughts down on paper can definitely be beneficial to your healing process!

I pray that each day, for the next 21 days, *Ebb & Flow* will be your healing companion as you embark upon your journey to a healthy heart and healthy relationships.

It's Okay to Not Be Okay

DAILY AFFIRMATION

"It's okay to be human and acknowledge when I am hurting."

EBB

Deep within all of us is a need to be loved, valued, and cared for by those with whom we are connected. We all want to be comforted in knowing that our relationships mean something and that each person is working hard in the relationship to ensure that needs are being met and desires are being fulfilled. We all want to know that we are important and that our heart will be taken care of by those we love and those who say they love us.

But what do we do when our life and relationships don't turn out the way we want? What do we do when our lives are turned upside down and our hopes are deflated from failed expectations and relationships gone bad? What do we do with the trouble we find ourselves in as a result of broken hearts and broken relationships?

Trouble is the deep emotional experience we have when life takes a U-turn and doesn't pan out the way we hoped. Trouble takes us to an unfamiliar place where we are forced to deal with our feelings in a way we had not anticipated. It catches us by surprise and requires us to look at our lives through a different set of lenses.

Many times, we have no reference point for the circumstances we face. We have no clue about how we got there or what led us to this place. With broken hearts, we search high and low for the reason we hurt and why our lives are in such disarray. It is in times like these we wonder if we will ever be okay again. We wonder if we will ever be able to pick up the broken pieces of our life and move forward. We wonder if we will ever find peace from the raging storms within.

FLOW

One of the things I have found out about life is that pain, disappointments, sadness, and heartache will come. As much as we try to avoid it, we will encounter storms over and over again in our lives.

Now, this is not to scare you or make you think that life will never be okay, because I believe it will. But, if we are going to make it through the storms of life, we must approach it from a balanced view and a positive perspective.

Trouble in the storm, as bad as it may seem, sets the tone for the impending greatness that is yet to be discovered in our lives. In fact, I would agree with the popular view that it is in our weakest moments that we find our strength. It is in the times of uncertainty we find a faith and confidence we didn't know we had before. It is in troublesome times we find that our pain is superseded by a

7

promise that there is a brighter day to come and, if we will endure the fight, there is victory on the other side.

Before you know it, you will find that pain has a purpose and that purpose is to enlarge your mental, spiritual, and emotional capacity to deal with life in a new way. It is in these times, you learn to adjust yourself to whatever life may bring and use it to propel you into your destiny.

The best part of it all is you learn that trouble does not last always. It is often used as a tool to sharpen your faith and anchor your soul through the highs and lows and the ebb and flow of your life and relationships. You learn to remain steadfast in your stance to endure the fight and continue moving forward, whether you have a solution to your problem or not.

The point I am making here is that trouble will come knocking at the door of all of our heart at some point and time in our lives. It is up to us to decide how we are going to deal with it when it comes.

When trouble does come knocking at the door, I believe one of the most important things we can do is remind ourselves that it's okay to not be okay. It's okay to be human and to acknowledge when we hurt. It's okay to say, "I'm overwhelmed and need time to pull away and allow myself time to repair from the damage that has been done to me."

When we process in this way, we take the pressure off of ourselves to try to be "superhuman" and prove that we have it all together. We release ourselves from trying to be something or someone we are not. Instead, we recognize our own limitations and lean on our faith to overcome the trouble we are facing, allowing God to do what only He can do. Doing so will give us the confidence we need to pick up the broken pieces of our life and move forward.

Something powerful happens when we understand that trouble is inevitable. But when it comes, we can acknowledge our brokenness and let go of the pressure to always feel we have to be okay. If we will allow ourselves the time we need to process through our pain, little by little, we can begin to pick up the broken pieces of our life and recover from the damage of a broken heart and broken relationships.

Reflections & Insights

Talk about an area of your life in which you are experiencing trouble. What are you facing and how does it make you feel?

_____

_____

_____

_____

_____

_____

_____

_____

_____

_____

_____

_____

_____

_____

_____

_____

Broken Pieces

DAILY AFFIRMATION

"I will move forward in the presence of my pain!"

EBB

Our relationships are characterized by the strength of the bonds we form with those we love. We can't always predict or guarantee the outcome of our connections. But one thing we know for sure is the enormous effect they have on our mental, spiritual, and emotional well-being. You see, our relationships serve as an environment by which we can either be strengthened or broken. It is within this context we learn to love, trust, and experience joy in our heart, peace in our mind, and rest in our soul.

But what happens when our heart breaks? What happens when we feel the pain of broken promises, lost hope, and unmet needs in our life and relationships? What happens when we feel isolated and alone because someone decides to disregard us and treat us as if we are unimportant?

When our heart breaks, the hurt we feel goes far beyond physical damage. The real damage is felt in the core of our being and deep in our soul. Our sense of joy, peace, and happiness is broken to the point where we no longer feel safe to be who we are and reveal our true selves for fear of further damage to our wounded heart, mind, and soul.

When our relationships break, the waters of our heart begin to ebb, as we struggle to find the means by which we can restore the love we once had.

When our heart breaks, we lose our excitement for life and our hope diminishes. We struggle to find the motivation we need to pick up the broken pieces of our heart and move forward.

I believe most of us would do better if we knew better. But many times we lack the understanding we need to resolve our pain and deal with the hurt we feel on the inside. We struggle with unanswered questions because we do not know how to trust again or when it is safe to love again. We may even hide who we really are because it frightens us to think that we might subject ourselves to further damage due to someone else's lack of love and concern.

But I am convinced that there are ways to pick up the broken pieces of our heart and become complete and whole again.

FLOW

Recovery from a broken heart means we must be willing to work through the hurt we feel on the inside when people and circumstances do not measure up to our expectations. We must be willing to make a conscious decision to keep moving forward, even if it means doing so in the presence of our pain. We have to decide how much we will allow the disappointment of failed relationships to affect our thoughts about who we are and our ability to trust again, believe again, and hope again. Yes, we get to decide how much we are going to allow our pain to hold us back from being able to find peace again in our life and relationships.

One way we can do so is by having the willingness to pick up the broken pieces of our heart and be strengthened again. We do this by connecting ourselves to people we trust and those who create a safe environment for us to process through our pain and open the door for us to love again. These are people who have no hidden motives or selfish ambition. They truly care about who we are and our ability to thrive in life. They are our most trusted friends and faithful confidants.

Picking up the broken pieces of our heart will require some work, a little bit of time, and a whole lot of God to lead us to the right people who can help us recover and heal from a wounded soul.

Yes, it will be hard, but it can definitely be done!

~~~≈≥≈~~~

Reflections & Insights

What "pieces" of your heart are broken right now? Who in your life can help you rebuild your love, hope, and trust again?

_____

_____

_____

_____

_____

_____

_____

_____

_____

_____

_____

_____

_____

_____

_____

_____

God & Time

DAILY AFFIRMATION

"I will allow God and time to help me create and nurture great relationships."

EBB

Broken hearts lead to broken relationships. Broken relationships make us feel lost and off-balanced. We get thrown into confusion when we find ourselves connected to people who are not good for us. These are people who make us feel less than who we are because they have little respect for the relationship-building process. Oftentimes, they could care less about hurting others and more about exalting themselves. I call it being self-centered.

Unfortunately, we find ourselves connected to people who only see life one way—their way. In their mind, everyone is wrong and they are right. They justify everything they do with the thought that everyone else just needs to get it together.

I have a little sticky note on my planning board at home that says, "God cares about how we treat people." This is something that came to my realization after having been treated very poorly by people I thought truly cared about me. I felt the sting of their disapproval when I decided I would not be ruled by their thoughts and opinions of me and go ahead and do what I knew was right according to what God wanted me to do. When I took this stand, I immediately felt these people trying to stand on top of me and minimize who I was and who God created me to be.

From this experience, I learned that stepping on everyone else to accomplish what we want in life is a dangerous thing because we are doing so to people who are deeply loved by God. No matter what we do in life, we must always remember the golden rule, "Treat others the way we want to be treated." We set ourselves up to be reckoned with when we treat people less than the way we should, which is with love, kindness, care, and concern.

Unfortunately, many of us are connected to people who see life selfishly through their own lens. They seek to minimize who we are by rejecting us and making us feel less than who we were created to be. If we allow ourselves to continue to stay connected to them, we will be greatly impacted by their negative thoughts and actions toward us and begin to lower our own self-worth by conforming to their thoughts and opinions.

I believe this is why so many people go back to unhealthy relationships. They tend to do so because they do not anticipate the enormous amount of emotional work that has to be done to detach from a bond that is built on dysfunction. Letting go of that bond is hard work and, many times, can only be done with two very important ingredients—God and time.

FLOW

God works in mysterious ways. He speaks ever so gently to our heart and shows us the purpose people serve in our life, how we should treat them, and how we should expect to be treated by them. He brings to light relationships that are good for us and those that are bad for us and helps us understand the difference between the two.

God, in His own time, and through His infinite wisdom helps us to understand how to decipher which relationships are beneficial to us and which will ultimately hold us back from being all that we can be.

He helps us to see to that bad relationships are those that are one-sided, rushed, and shallow. They take us to a place of brokenness, isolation, and a feeling of being incomplete and alone. They make us feel sad and hopeless on the inside.

On the other hand, God shows us the quality of good relationships. They are mutual. All parties are connecting on a deeper level. These relationships develop over time and are full of meaning and connection. They strengthen us and carry us through the tough times of life. They comfort our heart and bring us to a place of wholeness and healing. They make us feel good about ourselves on the inside and give us a sense of hope and promise for the future.

Time is our best friend because it allows us to slow down and think about who we are, where we are, and where we are going in life. It helps us avoid getting so deeply involved in poor relationship habits that we lose our sense of direction and become used to dysfunction. Easing into and out of relationships gives us an opportunity to make small decisions along the way that lead to the big decisions in the end.

In short, God tells us who we are and reminds us that our life is not only defined by our relationships with others, but more importantly, by our relationship with Him. In time, He will help us to discern the purpose each person serves in our life and the part they play to enrich us and help us become all that we have been created to be! He helps us to see that good relationships will add to us and not take away from us. They will extend our focus because they inspire us to celebrate who we are and the gifts and talents God has given to us to share and enjoy!

~~~

Reflections & Insights

What can you do today to nurture a great relationship in your life?

_____

_____

_____

_____

_____

_____

_____

_____

_____

_____

_____

_____

_____

_____

Make Good Decisions

DAILY AFFIRMATION

*"I get to decide how much
influence I will allow others to
have in my life and
relationships."*

EBB

As the Earth rotates on its axis, it bends in response to the opposing forces of the sun and the moon on its surface creating the low tide and the high tide.

Our thoughts, much like the ocean's tide, are also influenced by outside forces that pull them in one direction or another. Our thinking is influenced by the things that occur in the world around us. Our perception of these occurrences and the meaning we ascribe to them are critical to our ability to make good decisions for our life and relationships.

Thinking occurs from two different perspectives—our mental capacity ("thinking" with our head) and from our emotional capacity ("thinking" with our heart).

Case in point, when I am talking to someone, I hear the words they are saying to me and my mind is processing the information. Based on what I am hearing, I begin to feel a certain way. So, the thoughts I have in my mind elicit feelings based on what I believe in my heart about what the person is saying.

Practically speaking, when we believe someone loves us, we typically respond to them in a way that says, "I am connecting with someone who has my best interest at heart." We tend to respond to them in a positive way because we feel this person is in our life to help us, not harm us. When we connect with them, we feel safe and have a general sense of emotional security and well-being. We know they mean us well and, again, we believe they are in our life to help us, not harm us. So, our actions toward people have much to do with what we believe about them in our head and how we feel about them in our heart.

FLOW

You might ask, "What does all of this have to do with relationships?" Well, in my opinion, what we believe in our heart about people is the measuring stick by which we can determine how much we want to be involved with them. If someone has hurt us over and over again, we must take a moment to look inside to evaluate our beliefs about who they are and how much influence we will allow them to have in our lives.

When we find ourselves suffering from a broken heart over and over again in our relationships, I believe we must assess our beliefs about the person and the relationship. Are they leading us to health or are they leading us to brokenness? If it is the latter, I believe we should consider one of three options with respect to other factors that might be present in the situation:

1) *Remain in the relationship,* making no changes in our thoughts or actions, and continue to expose ourselves to the constant hurt they impose on us,

2) *Change the dynamics of the relationship* by changing our thinking about the purpose the person and the relationship serve in our life, and/or

3) *Exit the relationship altogether,* learn from our mistakes, and move forward.

What you decide to do in your relationships is your decision to make. You get to decide how much or how little you will allow your life to be influenced in a positive or negative way.

Remember, people can make you feel valuable or devalued. Those who try to take away your value, will pull you toward a life of sadness, pain, and strife. People who add value to your life will pull you toward greatness. They will complete you, not compete with you. When given the opportunity, they will do everything in their power to help you succeed. These are people who create a kind of pull that results in a floodgate of blessings in your life and relationships and take you to heights unknown!

Keep in mind that, the decisions you make about your connections today can have a huge impact on the ebb and flow of your relationships tomorrow! The better you can discern which relationships are good for you and those that are not beneficial to you, the better you can establish emotional stability and improve your overall quality of life and relationships.

I invite you to take a moment to think about the relationships you hold dear to your heart. Do they move you toward peace, joy, and happiness or do they hold you back from experiencing all that life has to offer? If it is the latter, then you have some important decisions to make.

Today, I encourage you to evaluate your thinking and make decisions that will help heal your heart and strengthen your soul. Good decision-making is essential to your recovery from a broken heart and broken relationships.

~~~

Reflections & Insights

*Think about someone who adds value to your life. Name
3 things you like about that person and how they make you
feel. Are you able to apply these characteristics to other
relationships in your life?*

DAY FIVE

Get Rid of PQRs

EBB

As you gear up to make important decisions about your life and relationships, keep in mind that changes will be necessary. I believe that, in order to move in any direction in life, you must prepare yourself for change and growth. That means you have to be willing to let go of the negative and grab a hold of the positive. You must surround yourself with positive people who have a great attitude and a renewed outlook on life.

Not only is it important to surround yourself with positive people, you must also be willing to rid yourself of the excess baggage that collects as a result of what I call PQRs.

PQR stands for "poor quality relationships." These are relationships that are not exactly stormy, but they do not add any value to your life. PQRs are relationships characterized by issues that are far more subtle, yet extremely damaging to your soul. These are relationships you might have with people who smile at you, but secretly relish in your demise. They do not want anything good to happen to you, through you, or for you.

PQRs occur with people who like you as long as they feel they are above you. As long as you do not supersede them in fame, fortune, beauty, class, or status, you're okay.

30

But the moment you reach down inside of yourself and begin to function within the gift that God has given you, they don't like it. Many times, people who foster PQRs will set out to intentionally sabotage you and hinder you from moving forward in life.

Beware, because these people can be those who say they love and support you, but secretly hate you because you have, in some way, challenged them to take another step toward their own destiny...one they often do not want to take.

I am always skeptical of those who say, "I love you", but their actions prove differently. I believe what they deem as love is really admiration which, if left unchecked, will spill over into envy. Because they do not want to take the necessary steps to become what God designed them to be, they want to keep everyone else from doing the same.

The envy we feel from people in PQRs can play on our thoughts, feelings, and emotions and lower our self-esteem. If we are not careful, we will begin to sink back into status quo simply because we seek their approval. Because we fear their disapproval, we conform to what they want instead of being true to ourselves and doing what we want and being who God created us to be.

FLOW

To overcome PQRs, we must be willing to release them. We must be willing to cut away the excess and let go of those who want to take from us, but never give anything back to us. These kind of people will drain you dry and steal the very life out of you!

I disagree with those who say you should give without expecting anything back. Although I do understand that what they are really encouraging us to do is avoid giving out of selfish gain, I believe we must still expect reciprocity in our relationships. Otherwise, it is not a healthy relationship. Moreover, I believe not only should our relationships be reciprocal, they must also be rewarding.

The reality of it is, if our relationships are going to prosper, they must come with some benefits and rewards. They should give us a sense of security knowing that whatever happens, the other person has our best interest at heart. Each person in the relationship is striving every day to ensure that they are a blessing to the other, never a hindrance or roadblock.

As I am writing this text, I ran across a social media post with a quote that says, "There comes a time when you have to stop crossing oceans for people who wouldn't even jump puddles for you." Wow, what a true statement! If someone in your life says they love you, but are not willing to fill your cup and make an investment in your life, this is a sign of a PQR.

Today, I want you to evaluate your connections and note the quality of your relationships. If people are not adding to your life, they are taking something away. Get rid of the excess baggage produced in PQRs and commit to spending more time with others who genuinely love, honor, respect, and support you.

In addition, recognize your own worth and value. Love who you are and surround yourself with people who will do the same. It is only when you engage and invest in relationships with people who are giving you the best of who they are, will you be able to enjoy the best of who you are and the beauty of real, authentic, high-quality relationships!

Reflections & Insights

Do you have PQRs in your life? What are your choices in dealing with this kind of relationship? (Refer back to the "Making Good Decisions" section for help.)

_____

_____

_____

_____

_____

_____

_____

_____

_____

_____

_____

_____

_____

_____

_____

_____

Love Anyway

DAILY AFFIRMATION

"I am willing to take the first step to express my appreciation to those I love."

EBB

One of my favorite reads is a mini-book written by speaker and Bible teacher, Joyce Meyer entitled "Do It Afraid." I love this book because it serves as a reminder that, anything I do in life (that is of any significance), is going to require me to do it in the presence of fear, doubt, discouragement, pain, and insecurities.

This concept of overcoming obstacles reminds me of the Apostle Peter in the Bible when he began to walk on the water toward Jesus. He was doing fine until he allowed his fear of the enormous winds and waves get the best of him. He took his eyes off of faith and began to fear. The moment fear set in, he began to drown.

In her book, Joyce reminds us that God has great things in store for us. Yet, just as with Peter, God doesn't always take us out of the storm. Instead, He gives us the tools we need to endure the storm and overcome any obstacles standing in our way.

I believe Joyce's 'do it afraid' concept also applies to our relationships. All too often we wait until the person who has hurt us apologizes or does something to make us feel better before we are able to forgive them. We live to hear "I'm sorry" or "I didn't mean to hurt you." But, all too often, our expectations of an apology are met with complete silence. The apology we long to hear never comes and we are left broken, wounded, and without resolution.

Releasing people from the hurt they have caused us, not only heals us, but it frees the other person. With the spiritual element of who we are, we can love them anyway because we recognize the fact that our self-worth and value does not lie with them. It is found in our faith in God and our decision to move forward, despite the hurt they have caused us.

Thinking back to the earlier part of my co-parenting relationship with my son's father, I remember being so upset with him because I didn't feel he valued me as a person. I didn't feel he appreciated me for all of the work I did on my own to parent our son. Because he wasn't there on a daily basis, much of his thinking about who I was, was based on what he saw outwardly, not who I was inwardly. This frustrated me because, for a long time, he couldn't see who I really was. He couldn't see my heart.

To overcome this frustration, I had to release myself from trying to prove to him that I was a good person. I had to move on and do what I needed to do to be a great parent to our son. I decided to love my son's father anyway, despite his feelings toward me and his thoughts about our relationship. I owned my part and I let him own his part. I settled in my mind that I was going to love him for who he was and that was it...end of story. If anything else was going to be accomplished, God would have to do it.

FLOW

It wasn't until later in our co-parenting relationship, that I learned this "love anyway" concept. As time went along, I began to realize that sometimes you have to be willing to move on with life and love people on credit. In other words, the relationships you value and decide to keep in your life might require you to love people when they themselves are not exactly loveable. You might be forced to communicate and interact with them, all at the same time they are getting on your nerves!

Herein lies the epitome of love!

Let me be clear, however, that these are not PQRs. No, these are people who genuinely love you, but may be experiencing some challenges in their own life that are somehow negatively affecting yours.

The test is can you take a chance and wade out into deep waters and love them anyway? Can you go ahead and have a conversation with them without needing someone to prompt and prod you to take the first step? Can you lay down your pride for just one moment to love and accept the person simply for who they are and not for who you think they should be?

Make up in your mind that you will resist the temptation to hide behind your disappointments and withhold your love from those who matter to you and you matter to them. The fact is, if God has forgiven you, then it is required that you forgive them. Don't wait to love those people in your life who you value, love, and respect. Don't put off apologizing to them if you have hurt them in any way. Compliment them and express how much they mean to you and the gift they bring to your life and to the relationship.

Something incredible happens when we decide to take the first step to just do it...to love people and to express that love in a way that is meaningful and healing for the soul.

Now, I want to be clear...just because we love, accept, and appreciate others for who they are, does not mean we allow them to wreak havoc in our lives. We must set boundaries and clear expectations for how we want to be treated. But those boundaries are set with the intention to improve and refine the relationship we have with them, not to tear it down.

Today, resolve to do what you can to take a step in the direction of your destiny. Let the momentum of your faith push aside your fear and make the way for you to experience the beauty of those who have been placed in your life for you to love and enjoy.

So, the next time you find yourself troubled over a relationship you truly value, let go of the hurt, love the person on credit, and *do it afraid*!

Reflections & Insights

Name 1 person you will commit to love despite their flaws. In loving them, what boundaries do you need to set?

_____

_____

_____

_____

_____

_____

_____

_____

_____

_____

_____

_____

_____

_____

_____

Forgive Yourself

DAILY AFFIRMATION

"I will free myself from perfection and accept who I am, mistakes and all!"

EBB

U^p to this point, we have addressed ways to deal with the brokenness we experience in our relationships with other people. But how do we reconcile the inner conflicts we have when we make mistakes and have trouble forgiving ourselves? What do we do when we know that it was our own choices and actions that knocked us off course?

Many times, we treat ourselves in the same way we would treat our own worst enemy. We hold ourselves to such an unreasonably high standard that we allow no room for error. We forget that, we too, are subject to mistakes. We all have shame and guilt in our past that we must be willing to release.

Not only that, but when we make mistakes, we oftentimes wrestle with the thought of what others might think about those mistakes. For some reason, we buy into the misconception that, how people feel about us, is how we should feel about ourselves.

With all due respect, I beg to differ!

Our self-esteem cannot rest on the opinions of others. Our confidence in who we are cannot be subject to the volatility of someone else's thoughts. Unfortunately, the way people feel about us ebbs and flows with the changing of the tide. One day they love us and the next day they despise us. Their feelings about us are too unstable to base our entire existence on them.

My advice?

FLOW

Forgive yourself and resist the internal struggle you might feel when someone holds you hostage to a higher standard than you can live up to. Instead, set your own standard and allow yourself time to grow and become the person you were designed to be. Do not allow negative thoughts about yourself and the negative opinions of others to take precedence over the positive thoughts you should have of yourself.

Love yourself, forgive yourself, and let go of the mistakes of your past. It's over. Move on and celebrate the beauty that is inside of you. Give yourself the time you need to grow and become the best person you can be!

45

~~~⚬~~~

Reflections & Insights

In what area of your life are you struggling to forgive yourself? What is 1 step you are willing to take to begin the process of letting go of your past and embracing your future?

_____

_____

_____

_____

_____

_____

_____

_____

_____

_____

_____

_____

_____

_____

_____

Be Comfortable in Your Own Skin

DAILY AFFIRMATION

"I am satisfied with who I am and love the person I am becoming!"

EBB

I am amazed at the shocking number of people who take their own lives every year because they reached a place of hopelessness or did not feel their life was important enough to see what was on the other side of their pain. My heart breaks to know that they found themselves alone in their struggle and locked in a prison of despair. They found themselves drowning in the sea of trouble without the life raft of hope to save their wounded soul.

Oh, how I wish they knew how valuable they were to life! I wish they knew how important they were to the lives of those who would need them further down the road. Unfortunately, they lost hope. They lost their connection and the will to fight to stay alive. Somehow, their view of the problem in front of them was clouded by feelings of helplessness, pain, and despair.

Our society heralds those who are beautiful, smart, wealthy, and strong and those who seem to have it all together. We gasp at the very thought of anyone who is anything less than the image we have in our minds of people who have it all together. I believe this is why so many people find themselves in troublesome situations. They are looking for an outlet. They long for the opportunity to simply be human—to laugh, cry, be angry, be sad, and simply express themselves without anyone judging them for doing so.

FLOW

I reject this demand for 'super-heroism'. If we are going to survive the tough stuff in life, we must take off the mask, embrace who we are, and seek to be comfortable in our own skin. We must love ourselves despite others' thoughts and opinions of us.

When we take our focus off of what others think about us and turn it to what we think about ourselves and how God views us, we soon learn that we are on a mission and that mission is too big to allow anything or anyone to get us off course. Instead of being worried about what others think, we must learn to appreciate our own worth and value. The more we appreciate who we are, the greater chance others will do the same. And, even if they do not, we are still okay.

When you are comfortable in your own skin, you no longer seek the approval of others because you recognize that rejection is a part of life. You understand that you will not fit in with everybody. Everyone will not accept you and appreciate you for who you are and what you bring to the table. In fact, some people will outright ostracize you just for being you. But let me remind you that, for every person who rejects you, this is one person's opinion out of over *7 billion other people* who exist in the world. There are a wealth of people who are willing to love you just as you are! There are people who will take the time to get to know you and not prejudge you. They will support you and accept you. They will not tear you down, but they will seek to build you up and be your strength in times of trouble. They will be your anchor in the storms of life and give you the mental, emotional, and spiritual encouragement you need to keep on keeping on!

If anything needs to be corrected in your life, they will give you constructive feedback that will help you grow and become even greater than you were before. Not only that, but they will affirm you and remind you of the incredible blessing you are to them and to life.

I invite you to take a look at yourself and appreciate the blessing you are to life. Appreciate your gifts and talents. Celebrate your successes. Invest in yourself. Believe in yourself and your ability to produce great fruit in your life and relationships!

If you have to establish new relationships to align with the positive thoughts you have of yourself, do it! It is well worth the effort! There is no better feeling than to live life surrounded by those who are comfortable with who they are and encourage others to do the same! When this happens, you know you are in the right place, with the right person, doing the right thing, at the right time!

Reflections & Insights

List 3 things you appreciate about yourself and why.
(Don't be shy!)

_____

_____

_____

_____

_____

_____

_____

_____

_____

_____

_____

_____

_____

_____

_____

_____

_____

The Quiet in the Storm

DAILY AFFIRMATION

"My peace is found in the middle of my storm!"

EBB

A storm is defined as a disturbed state of environment marked by significant disruptions to normal conditions. Typically, storms cause major damage to the people and things living in the environment in which it occurs. It is often unexpected in its approach and unforgiving in its regard to whatever is in its pathway.

The storm we experience on the outside is analogous to the storm that occurs on the inside of us. As we work our way through the ebb and flow of life, we might find ourselves dealing with issues that cause major disruptions deep in our soul leaving us feeling broken and alone. The winds and waves of disappointments that occur in our life can cause major disturbances in our heart as we struggle to find peace in the middle of the storm.

Pain results from the storms we face in life. It affects everything we know to be true and normal in our world. Pain causes disruption and demands change. It provokes us to adjust our thinking to embrace a new normal as we grapple with the disappointment of failed relationships and the reality of unmet needs. Pain occurs in the "ebbing" phase of life where we feel we are on the decline. We feel we have no power to overcome the situation we are facing. Without notice, life begins to spiral out of control as we wrestle with questions that have no foreseeable solutions. We begin to doubt our ability to handle the raging storms within as they seem to be bigger than our ability to overcome them.

FLOW

But there is a place in the storm that has major significance. It's called the "eye" of the storm. The eye is the center of the storm where the barometric pressure is the lowest making it a place of stillness and calm. The eye is a place where the skies are clear and there are little to no disturbances.

In practical terms, our soul is the center of who we are. It is the place deep within us that, if protected, is not easily moved or shaken by life's circumstances. It is a place where unrest and confusion cannot reside. Strife and heartache cannot take residence here because peace, love, and healing have made it home.

I believe there is a voice inside each of us that leads us to this place. The voice (which I call the Holy Spirit) guides us to the eye where we are not affected by the elements of the storm. This is the place where we are not moved by our circumstances because we have the tools we need to find our center and remain there until the storm is over.

In order to get to the center, or eye, of the storm, I believe we must be willing to do three very important things: stop, look, and listen.

Stop

Things happen in our life that are well beyond our control. When they occur, we must resist the urge to get into our "fix it" mode. No matter what we say, do, think, or feel, there are some things that happen in our life that we will not be able to change or fix. This is the time, we must lay down our pride and recognize that we are not God. We must recognize there is a bigger plan at work and be willing to take the pressure off of ourselves to fix the problem and overcome the storm on our own.

It is in these times, we must learn to *stop* trying to manipulate the situation, get out of the way, and let the storm pass. Of course, letting go in this way takes a lot of time and practice. But, if we are going to get through the raging storm within, we must be willing to allow for the natural order of things to take place as they are divinely designed to do so. As we let go of our need to be in control and hold on to the faith that everything will turn out exactly as planned, we will experience the ebb and flow of life according to God's will and in His timing.

Look

As the storm takes its course, we must be willing to view it from the right perspective. When we examine our circumstances with an open heart and mind, we can then begin to understand how we found ourselves in the storm in the first place. This is definitely the time we must be honest with ourselves as we seek resolution through the lens of objectivity.

Instead of looking outward, we must be willing to take a good look inward to see if there is anything we could have done to avoid the storm or to help make the situation better. Let me be clear that this is not a fault-finding exercise, but it is one we can engage in to potentially help minimize our exposure to troublesome situations in the future. I believe that the better able we are to detect signs of trouble, the more equipped we can be to handle it when it comes.

Listen

As we take the time to see our circumstances with a heart of openness and honesty, we must also position ourselves to hear the voice within that guides us to a place of shelter from the storm. Finding this place is the goal of meditation. Meditation allows us to pull aside, let go of our own thinking, and focus on what is actually occurring in our life at that moment. *Listening* is an important aspect of this process as we must be willing to, not only stop and look at the situation for what it is, but be open to hear direction from God so that we can understand how to handle situations in a way that comforts our heart and heals our wounded soul.

Remember, the eye is a place of stillness and quiet deep within us where we are able to hear things that cannot be heard in the noise of the raging, turbulent storms. When we meditate and position ourselves in our center, we are then able to hear small nuggets of wisdom that broadens our understanding of the storm, release our pain in the storm, and hold on to the promises of our future as we move away from the storm.

Finding the quiet in the storm is an art and one that is well worth the time it takes to cultivate it. If we hang in there long enough, we will begin to understand what it takes to, not only find the quiet in the storm, but to actually *overcome* the storm. When we are willing to stop and find our center, we are then in position to see the storm for what it is and hear the inner voice that guides us to the other side of it.

Taking the time to meditate each day is an important part of this process as it will give us the peace we need to brave the storm when it comes and provide us the tools we need to overcome it in our life and relationships!

Reflections & Insights

What storms are you fighting? What happened to bring you to this place? What actions can you take to move yourself closer to your center?

Defeat the Giant Within

DAILY AFFIRMATION

"I will let go and let God be in control!"

EBB

Many of you know the story of David and Goliath and how David, who was an unassuming shepherd boy, found himself face-to-face with Goliath, the Philistine giant who was far bigger and stronger than he. David became angry when he heard Goliath provoking the children of Israel to come to battle. He was so passionate about freeing his people from Goliath's constant taunting, he volunteered to fight him. Small in stature, David knew he could not overtake Goliath with his physical strength. He knew that if he was going to win the battle against this giant, he would have to have a strategy. With a slingshot in his hand, David used his faith in God and his knowledge from past experiences in the wilderness to overcome his enemy.

Like David, we all find ourselves facing giants in our life that are far bigger than us. We encounter situations we cannot figure out and things that are beyond our control. We often find that our intelligence, will, mental prowess, money, and power are not enough to overcome our enemies.

Now, the enemy David faced was a person, but the enemy I speak of here are the enemies we fight within—

worry, fear, doubt, discouragement, depression, confusion, hopelessness, and defeat.

If we are facing giants within, the amount of physical strength we need to overcome them is irrelevant. The real strength is in understanding the battle and knowing how to win the war. This knowledge is golden because we certainly do not want to find ourselves fighting a battle where there is no opportunity to win.

I believe the trouble we oftentimes find ourselves in is only a "smoke screen" to a deeper problem. Yes, we may be going through trouble from outside influences, but these influences are eliciting feelings that become our real struggle. Fear of not being able to make it alone may result from a broken relationship. Discouragement may stem from not being able to find the love we seek in life. These issues, along with the amount of time we give attention to them, become our stumblingblocks. As stated earlier, overcoming the storm that results from these barriers depend on how quickly we can identify the problem and equip ourselves with the tools we need to overcome it.

For example, if your heart is broken because someone mistreated you in a relationship, it is a problem they have on the inside of them toward you. But, it becomes your problem when you allow fear, stress, and worry about what they did to you, to consume you. Instead, you must understand that everyone in this world will not like you or treat you in the manner you feel you should be treated.

Does their contempt toward you make you a bad person? Absolutely not! It simply means you must accept the way they feel and then decide if you want to feel the same way. If your feelings contradict theirs, then you must believe in yourself and the awesome ability you have to move forward in life, no matter their feelings or the circumstances.

Will you continue spending time worrying about what you did wrong to make them not like you? Or, will you settle in your mind that you are on a mission and that mission requires you to be focused on your future, actively pursuing your goals in life, and ready to receive the great things that are in store for you?

FLOW

Like David, understanding our weakness and identifying the real enemy is where patience and strategy are key. In order for us to win the battle and defeat the giants within, we must be willing to take a step back and consider three very important principles:

To understand the behavior

1) Release your control…you are in the situation to participate, not dominate,

2) Recognize there is always something to be learned, and

3) Understand that your battle is not always about you! It is a part of a bigger plan!

Release Your Control

One of the most valuable lessons I have learned in life is that I am not in control. The even bigger lesson is in understanding that someone else *is*! In my world, that someone else is God and He is in the driver's seat. He is in FULL control. When I am facing storms in my relationships and things are not going as well as I had planned, my struggle is not in fighting the battle. My struggle is in allowing Him to fight the battle for me. He does this by giving me a plan and strategy so I know how to approach the situation in a way that I can use the right tools to get the right results.

We must recognize we are not to dominate, lord over, and try to control what others say, do, think, or feel. Instead, we must always be mindful that there is one Lord

65

and His name is Jesus! If anything needs to be changed in someone else's life, He will do the changing. He will turn the situation whichever way He chooses and that way is always the best way for all parties involved!

Learn

Now just because we are not in the driver's seat, does not mean we do not have a valuable part to play in defeating our giants. The wisdom here is in recognizing the knowledge that is to be gained in the situation and understanding the special part we should play to acquire that knowledge and use it as a weapon to win the war. We must position ourselves to understand that there is wisdom to be gained in every situation—even as we stand face to face with our giants!

Understand the Bigger Plan

If we will take our time and allow our situations to unfold, we will realize we are continuously learning and growing. The battles we face might be the tool used to help us overcome deep-seeded fears, anxieties, hurts, pains, and disappointments that have been buried in our hearts that the situation itself is bringing to surface.

Not only that, but we will also understand that we are a part of someone else's growth process. In fact, many times the battle we face is, as they say, "iron sharpening iron." In other words, we are tools used in each other's lives that make way for old habits to be cut away and poor behaviors to be extinguished.

Understanding the bigger plan means we recognize that we are growing and our lives are being used to help others grow, as well. Knowing this, we can begin to overcome our fears and use our faith to win the battle.

We can look to David for our example. He was confident that he could overtake the giant, not because of his physical strength, but with the mental and spiritual strength he had been given by God. In facing Goliath, he knew God had already prepared him and would give him the tools he needed to win the battle, and ultimately, the war.

In the same way, God will give you the wisdom, knowledge, and tools you need to overcome your enemies and defeat the giants within!

Reflections & Insights

*Name 1 way you feel you are being used to help
someone else grow? How are they helping you grow?*

_____

_____

_____

_____

_____

_____

_____

_____

_____

_____

_____

_____

_____

_____

_____

_____

Synchronize Your Heart, Mind, Body, & Soul

DAILY AFFIRMATION

"I will align my heart, mind, body, and soul to speak the same language!"

EBB

Have you ever felt like life was really weird? Maybe you got some bad news, but somehow good came out of it. Or maybe you were experiencing the best time of your life, but there was something looming in the back of your mind that wouldn't allow you to fully enjoy the moment. You just got married, but you're still grieving the loss of a past relationship. You just broke away from a bad relationship, but now you're afraid to move on without your former significant other.

Such is the ebb and flow of life.

Alternating forces occur in our lives and relationships that tend to knock us off balance. We want to enjoy the blessings we have in life, but struggle to deal with the challenges we face in having them. We desperately want to live a great life and have great relationships, but fear, doubt, and discouragement often present roadblocks that hold us back from doing so.

So, what do we do? How do we handle these contradictions? How do we deal with the waves of uncertainty that creep up on us and prevent us from truly enjoying our life and relationships?

FLOW

I believe one of the things that helps us to cope with the contradictions of life is to approach it with a *pure heart* and from a balanced perspective. That means we deal with the troubling issues of our heart, yet still remain positive about our outcomes. We acknowledge our weaknesses, yet embrace our strengths. We accept our hurt, but strive to obtain our healing. In other words, we accept reality as it is, but continually strive to make it better. A pure heart is all about balance and creating an atmosphere whereby we can thrive in life.

Not only should we seek to have a pure heart, but we must also show consistency in our thinking. Success in our life and relationships typically requires us to have a *made up mind* about what we want and then take the necessary steps to move us toward our goal. This can be tough because our decision to pursue one thing or another may require us to give up some things (or people) that are inconsistent with the direction we choose to take. This can be scary because letting go will require us to take some sort of *action* to release the old so that we can obtain the new.

But, when our heart is pure we can be honest with ourselves about what we want and make up our mind that

71

we will let our actions do the work to obtain it. Believe you me, this is definitely easier said than done and may have to be done over time. But no matter how long it takes, it has to be done if we are seeking to align who we are with what we say we want out of life.

We must realize that many times our relationships are not moving in a positive direction because we say we want one thing, but our actions and behaviors speak of something different. In other words, our behavior is not consistent with what we say with our mouth, believe in our heart, and think in our mind.

For example, in our heart we might long for a great relationship with our significant other, and believe in our mind that we can have it. But, we engage in continual conflict with him or her that contradicts everything we say we want to achieve.

The question here is, if we say we want great relationships, do we do the things that are necessary to create them? Do we use kind words to show our compassion toward our significant other? Do we go the extra mile to ensure that our companion feels honored and respected in the relationship? Do we spend time with them and show how much we love and care for them? In other words, do our actions exhibit what we say we want for our relationships?

If so, great! That means our heart, mind, and body are in sync and our *soul* is experiencing the benefits of this synchrony. If not...well, we've got some work to do! The work is in understanding the time, effort, and attention that is needed to create alignment in our life and do what it takes to ensure that every part of who we are is in harmony with the goal we have set for ourselves and our relationships.

As stated earlier, great relationships are intentional and will require every part of our being to be in sync. Synchrony creates harmony and harmony creates a deep sense of connection and satisfaction that is evident in our heart, mind, body, and soul!

Reflections & Insights

What area of your life do you feel is out of alignment?
What can you do to get your heart, mind, body, and soul in
synchrony?

_____

_____

_____

_____

_____

_____

_____

_____

_____

_____

_____

_____

_____

_____

_____

_____

Take Time to Heal

DAILY AFFIRMATION

"I will let go of the pain in my heart and give myself the time I need to heal!"

EBB

W hen I speak of healing the human heart, many people ask very legitimate questions like, "How do I know when I am completely healed?" or "How do I know when I am ready to start a new relationship?" These are very valid questions and ones I think are worth exploring.

Healing refers to the repair of something that has been damaged or broken. The amount of healing we need to recover from a broken heart and broken relationships is dependent on how much damage has been done to the heart. When your heart is broken, it is important to take the time you need to understand what happened to create the situation and then be willing to keep your heart open so that it can be repaired.

Emotional damage occurs when needs like safety, security, and significance are not met. Feeling unsafe in relationships causes us to build walls around our heart and put up barriers when we feel we might experience further harm. We have a tendency to shut down and avoid opportunities to fully express how we really feel to others for fear of rejection. In this way, we suppress our feelings to the degree that we stop living, we stop loving, and, in essence, we become a human robot...simply performing daily duties, but not really living life to the fullest.

FLOW

From a personal perspective, when my heart is broken from a lost or strained relationship, I tell myself, "This pain cannot remain!" But in saying that, I know I have some work to do. It means I must bring myself to a point where I am willing to deal with the situation head on and be real with myself about how it made me feel. I have to own my part of the problem, accept responsibility for it, and then be willing to begin the healing process.

I believe one of the most important things we can do to heal from a broken heart and broken relationships is to *talk about it*. Problems can seem big until you open up and talk about them. The more you release your frustrations, hurt, and pain to someone else, the more the problem seems to get smaller and smaller.

Something magical happens when we release the brokenness in our heart and allow the hurt and pain to flow out of us. In this way, we are making room for healing to occur. Once we give away the hurt we feel on the inside, we can then begin to fill our heart with the love, comfort, and compassion it needs to heal.

77

In addition to talking with someone you know and trust about the wounds of your heart, I believe it is equally important to examine your *self-talk*. In other words, what are you saying to yourself about yourself? Are you spending time encouraging yourself on the inside or are you engaging in circular self-questioning tactics that keep you bound to the problem?

Positive self-talk can do wonders for the human soul as it helps to strengthen you on the inside. It takes the focus off of the problem and puts the attention on your own personal growth and healing.

Keep in mind that words are powerful. They have the ability to build us up on the inside and make us stronger in the process. The repair of our heart begins to take place as we become willing to talk about the hurt that has been dealt us and use words of affirmation to build us up and make us whole, healed, and healthy on the inside!

Reflections & Insights

Have you been holding on to pain? If so, who can you confide in to help you release your pain? If the answer is "no one", feel free to use the space below to express your thoughts.

_____

_____

_____

_____

_____

_____

_____

_____

_____

_____

_____

_____

_____

_____

Find Your Rhythm

DAILY AFFIRMATION

*"I will learn to take
the good with the bad
and go with the flow!"*

The word *rhythm* is defined as a strong, regular, repeated pattern of movement. Related to the tide in the ocean, water rises and falls in a rhythmic pattern. This rhythm is caused by the attraction to, or pull of, the moon on the earth's surface. As this attraction occurs, it bends the surface of the earth toward the moon causing a high tide. As the earth rotates away from the moon, the pull is not as strong and therefore gives way to the low tide.

Now, let's apply this concept to our life and relationships.

EBB

Just as the tide in the ocean rises and falls, so does the rhythm of our life. This rhythm, in my opinion, is determined by how well we can manage the ups and downs in our relationships and steady ourselves through it all. It is determined by how much we are willing to push to get what we want, yet wait until the timing is right to grab a hold of it. It is about balancing our thoughts and desires to manage the good with the bad and be okay through it all.

One thing we must be careful of is wanting something so badly that the force of the attraction pulls us well beyond our limits, tilting our lives out of balance.

This can be a dangerous thing because the desire to have something can be so strong that we will stop at nothing to get it. This kind of pull brings about such an obsession with the object of our desire that we lose our rhythm and sense of direction. We step over what we know to be true and right and go after what we want without any consideration of the impact it will have on us or other people.

I believe it is a normal thing for us to want to establish strong connections. However, when the desire for those connections becomes so overpowering that we lose our sense of balance, we set ourselves up for failure. Because we want the person or thing so badly, we become impatient and run the risk of trying to control the situation to get what we want. We lose our rhythm when we fail to wait for the right timing to obtain the right result. This is typically when we see worry, fear, and doubt taking residence in our heart and mind.

FLOW

To create a flow in our lives, we must avoid extremes and allow people to move in and out as needed. Although we might bond with our mate, spouse, or significant other, our existence cannot be defined by the presence or absence of any one person. As hard as it may be, we must understand that our life has a rhythm which makes us appreciate when things are up and be patient when things are down, knowing that life is unpredictable and can change at any given moment.

In relationships, there are times we might feel that the only way we can be connected to someone is in the way we want to be connected. But, mature thinking requires us to understand that we may not be able to get from the relationship what we want. However, we can choose to enjoy the parts of the relationship that are available for us to enjoy.

Again, this kind of thinking is not easy to embrace. But the freedom comes when we are able to take the good with the bad in relationships and seek to enjoy it all. We approach life from a more realistic standpoint when we are able to love people when they come and love them when they go. We maintain our balance when we refuse to be controlled by our feelings. Instead, we use our feelings to connect with those we love in a way that is balanced and real.

There is a comfort in finding our rhythm in life because it allows us to approach our situations from a poised perspective. We come to understand that circumstances will ebb and flow, but we can remain steady

84

as we go with the flow and align ourselves with the motion of the tide. Rhythm tells us when to hold on and when to let go and allow things to happen naturally and in their own time.

When we find our rhythm in life, we can sit back, relax, and enjoy our relationships!

Reflections & Insights

In what area might your life be out of rhythm? What are 2 ways you can bring it back into balance?

_____

_____

_____

_____

_____

_____

_____

_____

_____

_____

_____

_____

_____

_____

_____

DAY FOURTEEN

Present in the Moment

DAILY AFFIRMATION

*"Today, I will be thankful
for all of the blessings I have
in my life and
relationships!"*

EBB

Every day we live is one step closer to our exit from this earth. I know this sounds somewhat eerie, but death is a reality and something we will all have to face at some point and time in our life.

Thoughts of death give me a greater appreciation for life. I like to view it from the standpoint of hindsight. I think about how I want to feel in the end when I look back over my life to reflect on the things I have done and the people with whom I have done them.

My greatest fear is in looking back to realize I did not take advantage of the opportunities I had in front of me to spend time with those I love and do the things I was sent here to do. I shiver at the very thought of giving anything less than 100% of my heart, mind, body, and soul to the divine purpose for which I was created.

FLOW

All too often we look back to find the reason why our life is the way it is. Or we look toward the future wondering what will happen next. I believe both of these processes are necessary in order for us to take the next step forward in life. But before we lace up our shoes and get ready to embark upon the next phase of our journey, I believe it will help us to stop, just for a second, and be present in the moment.

Let's take a moment to appreciate all of the people in our life who have helped to shape and form us into who we are today. Let's pause briefly to acknowledge how blessed we are to be able to read this meditational guide and share it with others. Let's celebrate the gifts we have been given to pour into the lives of those we love, despite the problems we might be facing.

In the hustle and bustle of life, we often forget to take a moment to appreciate all of the wonderful blessings that have been given to us. Instead of looking at the negative, we must consciously fix our minds on the positive and show our gratitude for what we do have in life.

I am convinced that, when we stop to count our blessings, more will follow. It is only when we relax and enjoy our present moment, can we let go of the failures of our past and look forward to the promises of our future.

Now we are ready to strap on our shoelaces and take the next step into our destiny!

Reflections & Insights

Name 5 people you are thankful for today. How do they enhance your life?

Appreciate the Wait

DAILY AFFIRMATION

*"Patience helps me respect the
process while I wait."*

EBB

People of faith oftentimes have no problem understanding the idea that God is in control and that He is the ruler of all things. The very fact that we call ourselves "believers" mean we believe in something bigger than ourselves and that someone is in complete control.

But, no matter how strong our faith is, there are things we will encounter in life that will catch us off guard and completely knock us off course. Even though, mentally, we might understand that these circumstances are all a part of life, emotionally, it does not take away the sting we feel when troubling situations arise.

Although we believe that God will carry us through the storm and we will make it to the other side, sometimes life stills hurts. Despite our faith, we are still susceptible to the pain that comes with a broken heart and broken relationships. When we hurt, we feel the emotions that threaten to overshadow the hope we once had in building a good life and great relationships.

The important questions at hand here are "What do we do with our thoughts, feelings, and emotions that oftentimes scream defeat?" and "What do we do while we are waiting for our circumstances to get better?" "What do we do when we are dissatisfied with our life, but see no feasible way out?" *We know we want change, but don't know how to make that change happen.*

FLOW

I believe one of the most important things to remember when going through a test is that the situation we are going through is not only a test, but an opportunity to learn something new about ourselves that we did not know before.

The second thing we must remember is that our test is not just about us, it's about those we will meet later on in life who will need our story. They will need the encouragement, strength, and hope we have that things will get better. They need us to become living proof that the situation is not too big to overcome. The very fact that we made it through to the other side is a testimony of God's goodness in helping us overcome whatever situation arises in our life.

The things we learn "while we are waiting" are golden nuggets of wisdom that anchor us through the storm. This wisdom helps us to remain steady in troubled times and gives us the strength and mental fortitude we need to push through whatever circumstance life sends our way. Even with broken hearts and in broken relationships, there is still something we can share with those in need. In our time of waiting, we come to understand that the process is far more important than the outcome. It cannot be rushed. It is like fine wine that gets better with time. In the meantime, we learn about ourselves and how valuable we are to life. We learn that there are so many people who can and will be blessed by our very existence and life experiences.

That is why I am writing this meditational guide. I recognize that my experiences as a woman, mother, child, sister, and friend can help someone in need. My pain can be someone else's gain. My ebb can be someone else's flow.

Sometimes we don't know what we don't know. We may be thinking that our storm in life is just a nuisance and something we can definitely do without. But don't write it off just yet. Just because you don't understand the meaning of your trouble, does not mean it does not have significance.

I believe there is a purpose for everything we experience. We must understand that, the very fact that God allowed the trouble to occur in our lives, means He has a plan for it. With that being the case, we must resolve in our hearts that there is nothing we will go through that is designed to overtake us. Even though problems in life may seem bigger from the start, we must understand that, day-by-day, we are developing the wisdom, strength, and tenacity we need to overcome it.

After a while, we will begin to see that trouble is simply an indicator that we are well on our way to someplace great. If we are patient in the process, we will reap the benefits of our willingness to wait with hope in our hearts and love deep within the wellspring of our soul.

Reflections & Insights

Name 3 things you can do while you wait for your circumstances to change.

Push Forward

DAILY AFFIRMATION

"I will not quit in my pursuit of a great life and great relationships!"

EBB

My first book, SINGLE MOM, PHD was born out of my passion to tell my story and share the lessons I learned as a result of the hurt and pain I had experienced as a single mom. The intense emotional struggles I overcame in that process gave me the drive I needed to go out into the world and help other single moms who were striving to do the same.

Months and months went into writing the story, editing, publishing, and getting the book ready for print. I didn't have a lot of money, but I had a vision and a dream to help others who were going through similar life circumstances. I had a testimony burning on the inside of me that was waiting to come out. I wanted to let people know that, it's not what you see on the outside that matters. It's the strength and courage that is built on the inside that proves your perseverance through the process.

I remember going through situations where I didn't know where my help was going to come from or how I was going to make it through. I remember being hungry and not having enough food to eat. I remember being so tired from the lack of sleep, I would almost pass out from sheer exhaustion. But I learned that, if anything was going to get done, I had to push my way through it. Most importantly, I learned that I could win, if I didn't quit.

As scary as it seemed, the desire to survive the ebb and flow of single motherhood was bigger than my fear of drowning in the sea of despair. It was bigger than my insecurities and more significant than my shortcomings. I wanted to be free from the raging storms of life and was determined to do so at all cost.

FLOW

One of the most valuable things I have learned in my experience as a single mom is that freedom from broken hearts and broken relationships does not just happen. No, when you really want to be free, you have to be willing to push your way through the problems of life and deny yourself the right to quit. You have to say "no" to anger, disappointment, and despair and not allow them to rule over your thoughts and emotions. You have to not allow brokenness to keep you silent and make you feel isolated and alone.

There is an art to overcoming challenges in our life and relationships. I believe that the way we handle situations determines the length of time that is required for us to get through them. There are things I went through in my younger days that lasted for several years. Now that I am a bit older and wiser, the same situations I endured for years, may only last a day and sometimes even a few moments.

For example, I used to worry about not measuring up to the expectations of other people. As I have matured in life, I no longer look to others for validation and approval. I am confident in who I am and comfortable in my own skin. Because I no longer seek the approval of others, their disapproval is no longer an issue.

Most importantly, I have come to understand that I have a choice to make in how long I will allow a problem to be a problem in my life. I get to choose how long I am going to allow myself to deal with certain situations that do not align with my life's goals. I get to choose how much time and effort I will give to people or things that really do not benefit my life. I get to decide how much power I am going to give to any one person to control my thoughts, feelings, and actions. I get to decide how long I will allow the hurt from broken relationships to hinder me from moving forward.

Today, I challenge you to make a conscious decision to push forward in life and do what it takes to remove the barriers that are holding you back from experiencing a great life and great relationships!

Reflections & Insights

What choices do you need to make in life that will push you forward toward a great life and great relationships?

_____

_____

_____

_____

_____

_____

_____

_____

_____

_____

_____

_____

_____

_____

_____

_____

_____

_____

DAY SEVENTEEN

Love Yourself

DAILY AFFIRMATION

"I will love myself in the same way I love others!"

EBB

People who know me, know that when I embark upon a task, I do it diligently and with great fervor. In my opinion, there is no room for mediocrity or slack. The job is done with excellence, precision, and high quality from start to finish.

Now, this all sounds really good and works very well in my world, but not necessarily for everyone else. I am admittedly a very task-oriented person. But I quickly learned in life that people cannot be manipulated like tasks. People come with their own set of ideas, thoughts, and feelings. Unfortunately, these do not always align with our own beliefs and unique way of doing things.

Many times, we struggle internally when people are not like us or do not handle things in the same way we do. In relationships, we oftentimes experience a huge amount of stress when they do not measure up to the high level of expectations we set for them. We think something is "wrong with them" when they do not see life in the same way we do.

When others do not conform to our way of thinking, how we handle it is definitely the ground upon which our character is tested.

My pastor always says true character is found in how we treat other people...especially those we feel we don't need. When I am considering someone for any kind of partnership, I watch how they not only treat me, but how they treat other people. If the treatment of other people is unacceptable, I know there is the potential to treat me in the same manner. This greatly affects how deeply I allow myself to be involved with this person going forward.

FLOW

In order for us to flow in our relationships, I believe we must respect people for who they are and avoid trying to make them who we want them to be. No matter what situation we are in, whether business or personal, we must always be mindful that people belong to God, and not us. Therefore, their performance does not negate their position as God's child. So, we must always be ever-so-careful to treat them with love, kindness, gentleness, and respect. We must be humble in spirit, leaning on His wisdom to help us make the decisions we need to make that is best for all parties involved.

We must handle people from the standpoint that excellence is the standard. But we cannot crush their spirit when they fall short of meeting our expectations. Instead, we should help them understand what we want and allow them the opportunity to decide if they want to meet the standards we have set or do something different. And we must do all of this with much grace and unending mercies.

Why should we worry so much about how we treat other people?

I believe loving others despite their flaws is the same process we must take when we ourselves have failed to live up to our own expectations. When we operate at a level less than what we desire, we must accept ourselves for who we are and love ourselves through the process. It is only when we understand that we, too, are in need of grace and forgiveness, can we then extend that same grace and forgiveness to others. So, the better we love ourselves, the better we can love other people. These two concepts both go hand in hand!

Loving ourselves as we love others means we broaden our ability to extend grace and, at the same time, receive it. We do not put ourselves on a higher pedestal than others, nor do we diminish our own worth and value for their sake. There is a mutual respect for both parties involved in the relationship.

In short, we must always keep in mind that, how we love others, is a reflection of how we should love ourselves and vice versa!

Reflections & Insights

How are you loving yourself right now? In what ways can you extend that same love to someone else?

_____

_____

_____

_____

_____

_____

_____

_____

_____

_____

_____

_____

_____

_____

(Un) Solved Mysteries

DAILY AFFIRMATION

"Today, I will open myself to learn and seek a greater understanding of my life and relationships."

EBB

A bout five years ago, I was on vacation in Destin, Florida. I remember standing on the beautiful shore of the Atlantic Ocean trying to mentally take in the vast gulf of waters that were before me. How incredible it was to see the crashing of the waves and hear the sound of the seagulls as they flew above the water trying to find even ground.

The mere size of this huge body of water was breathtaking to say the least! It seemed as if there was no beginning or end and the ocean itself had become one with the heavens, having no limitations or restrictions. Because I had very limited knowledge of its actual size and depth, I certainly didn't have the skills I needed to wade out into this massive body of water to see what was out there to be discovered!

There was a certain mystery behind the ocean that fascinated me. It made me want to know more. It drew me in and peaked my curiosity. It was beautiful to admire, yet dangerous in its ability to completely consume anyone who would dare to approach it without respect to its overwhelming presence.

As I proceeded toward the water, I did so with caution to ensure that I was adequately prepared to be engulfed by the flood of waves that were crashing ashore! Not only did I consider the strength of this huge body of water, but I was also fascinated by the millions of creatures in it that call the ocean their home.

Recollection of my time in Destin brings to mind the feeling I get when I am up against something that seems too big for me to handle. Finding a solution to a problem in our relationships can be overwhelming and somewhat scary. The problem may seem so big that "wading out into the deep" can be extremely intimidating.

So, how do we overcome this mystery? How do we know what tools to use to survive the overwhelming problems we might be facing as we wade out into the deep waters of life?

Now, the answers to these questions are not easy to obtain because we live in a very complex world that places huge demands on us and requires us to deal with things for which we have no reference point. Because we lack the experience we need to resolve the issues, we oftentimes settle for defeat, thinking that there is no workable solution.

FLOW

Although there are some problems we encounter that may take us by surprise, I am convinced there are ways we can be prepared for the things that are too big for us to handle in life.

First, we must have *faith*. Faith is believing in something we cannot see with our naked eye, but we know it's there. And not only do we know it's there, but we behave in such a way that says "what I want is already present in my life, and I will act accordingly." So, our faith is exhibited not just in believing, but also in our doing. We must always remember that action is required in order for faith to work.

Secondly, the action we take must be in *alignment* with our desired goal. In other words, you cannot say you want a great relationship, if you are not willing to work to have it. This takes us back to the concept of synchrony. In essence, we must live life with consistency and continuity.

Let me give you an example. Many single people I know (including myself) say they want to be married or have someone special in their life. But their actions speak differently. Somehow, they tend to connect with other people they think are potentials only to find out these people do not exhibit signs of being a suitable lifelong partner. They do not show evidence of characteristics that are needed to create and maintain great relationships like commitment, perseverance, and teamwork. Because they choose to continue in these kinds of relationships, they continue to struggle, not recognizing that their actions do not align with what they say they want.

This brings me to my third point, which is having the willingness to embrace the reality of a *limited view*. Just as the ocean in all of its complexities must be respected for its vastness, so does life. Life comes with so many twists and turns that, a part of overcoming its challenges, is in acknowledging the fact that it's too big for us to know everything about it. Therefore, we must lean on the support and insight of God and others to help us navigate our way through it.

I don't believe any of us were born to do life by ourselves. With that said, we must humble ourselves enough to realize that our perspective has limitations. We do not see all of the intricate details needed for us to make solid decisions that determine our next step in life. So, we must allow God and other people to speak words of wisdom and encouragement to us that will help us move from the shore out into the deep waters.

I believe the key here is in understanding that there is always an answer to the problems we face in life. But we must be humble enough to recognize the fact that there are some things that are hidden from our awareness, and be willing to remain steady in the process until the mystery begins to unfold.

Have you ever gone through brokenness in your life and felt there was no solution in sight? As time went by, however, the answer began to reveal itself and you then understood so much more than you did before. You began to understand that your brokenness was a result of many things that were beyond your control or simply things you were not aware of.

Such is the essence of life experiences.

Everything we go through stems from the fact that we lack knowledge about things that are hidden from us, at first. But as we continue in the journey, the truth begins to unravel and reveal itself to us.

The vastness of the ocean is a huge reminder that there are so many facets of life waiting to be explored. We must remember this when we are experiencing situations we cannot figure out. If we will hold on to faith and remain patient in the process, the answers to our (un)solved mysteries will begin to unfold, in due time. We can then use this new knowledge to usher us further into a life filled with hope and a heart filled with love.

~~∞~~

Reflections & Insights

Think about a past relationship experience in which you lacked the knowledge of what to do? How did you gain the wisdom you needed to overcome the problem?

_____

_____

_____

_____

_____

_____

_____

_____

_____

_____

_____

_____

_____

_____

_____

_____

_____

Faith, Fidelity, & Finesse

DAILY AFFIRMATION

"Today, I will commit to healing and invest in my own personal growth and wellness!"

EBB

E nduring through life's struggles is no easy task. In fact, many things we go through lands many of us in the hospital, on our sick bed, or even at the morgue. Life is no joke. I often question those who pretend that they have it all together and then look at you with a critical eye when you begin to talk about the problems you might be facing in life.

In fact, while writing this meditational guide, many people questioned why I was writing a "relationship" guide, seeing that I have never been married. But, in my opinion, a wounded heart is a wounded heart whether you experience it within the context of a marriage, courtship, friendship, work relationship, death experience, or otherwise. Hurt is still hurt and something none of us wants to experience.

One day, while finishing up my daily run, I began to ponder what it takes to truly enjoy life again after having gone through a broken relationship. As I thought about it, three powerful tools came to mind—faith, fidelity, and finesse.

FLOW

Now, we have already talked about faith and the role it plays in helping us move forward in life. But, just as a

118

means of nailing it down, I want to reiterate its importance in our ability to, not simply move forward, but to truly enjoy our life and relationships in the process.

Faith

Faith is much like credit. You spend it without having the actual evidence of what you want, but you hang in there knowing that you're going to get it. Faith is a beautiful thing because it broadens our capacity and helps us experience things that are well beyond our own abilities. It reaches far beyond the acquisition of things. Faith takes us to a place where our very quality of life is enhanced. With faith, we become a "superhuman" knowing that we can overcome anything life throws our way (of course, all of this being accomplished with God's help!).

When our heart is broken, faith tells us to pick ourselves up and take one small step in the direction of healing. It also requires us to be grown up and not allow the little things in life to become stumblingblocks. It takes us to places where few people are willing to go. Faith helps us learn to discern to which things we need to attend to and the situations that are better left for someone else to fix. This leads me to my next point...fidelity.

119

Fidelity

One of the things I find to be the hardest to accomplish in life is the ability to "stay true to the game." Fidelity is defined as being loyal, faithful, and committed to becoming whole and healed in the process—even when we want to give up seeing no evidence of things getting better. It's one thing to say we want something, but it's another thing to maintain the endurance we need to obtain it.

The true test in life is, not only overcoming our challenges, but maintaining fidelity in the process. In other words, can you see the problem all the way through to the end and maintain a good heart and a great attitude in the process?

Finesse

Finesse is defined as having skill or expertise. In terms of relationships, finesse is illustrated when we can "take a licking and keep on ticking." It is living life with style and class, even when we know people are waiting in the wings to see us to fail.

Granted life is not always pretty. But when we are faced with extremely difficult situations in our relationships, the question becomes, "Can we avoid letting trouble sway us to do things that are outside of our character?" "Can we do the work we need to do behind the scenes to sharpen our skill and equip ourselves with the tools we need to go through the storms of life?"

One way we do this is by filling our heart and mind with the information we need to overcome adversity. Personally, I listen to inspiring music and read books that offer encouragement and hope. I keep God close to me through prayer and, as much as possible, I surround myself with people who can lift me up, and not tear me down.

My question to you is, "How do you sharpen your emotional skills?" "What helps to strengthen your heart in times of grief and sorrow?" What anchors you when life begins to ebb and flow and the winds and waves come crashing down on you?

I challenge you today to begin the process of healing by strengthening yourself through whatever channels help to build you up and remind you of your significance in life. Reading this meditational guide is one of the ways you can start on your journey to freedom and open your heart to be whole, healed, and healthy again.

Let it encourage you and help you endure the raging storms within. Let it motivate you to live your life with faith, fidelity, and finesse!

Reflections & Insights

Name 3 tools you can use to strengthen your heart and mind as you go through the storms of life?

Uniquely You!

DAILY AFFIRMATION

"I appreciate myself and the unique gift I bring to life!"

EBB

I love people. I believe the complexity of who we are as human beings is fascinating. Every part of our existence breathes of deity. We are not one dimensional. It is evident that every aspect of who we are is carefully and meticulously crafted and woven together to create a masterpiece. As humans, we have potential. We have strength. We have the capacity to be…and with that comes all sorts of possibilities.

Our very existence speaks of purpose. We are here for a reason. We rise up every morning with a mission to accomplish something greater than ourselves. We set out every day to see what the day will hold for us and what challenges we can overcome.

But what makes us special? What is it about each of us that makes us different from any other human being?

I know this question has been pondered since the beginning of time. But for my own purpose, I wanted to know first-hand what others might think.

To answer this question, I took to social media and posed two questions, "What makes you unique?" and "What makes you proud to be you?" Needless to say, I received some very insightful feedback. One person responded and said "being comfortable in your own skin is what sets you apart from everyone else." Another said they enjoy learning from others and incorporating what they learn in their own life.

FLOW

I think both points are genius and I agree with both. I believe when we remain true to who we are and celebrate our own gifts, strengths, and talents, it is then we can truly begin our healing process and allow ourselves to become who we were created to be day-by-day.

So I ask you the same question, "What makes you unique?" "What makes you different from anyone else on this Earth?"

Now you may be wondering why I am talking about the uniqueness of who you are in a book that is about recovering from broken hearts and broken relationships. I feel it is important to address who you are because the better you understand yourself, the better you understand other people. The more you appreciate yourself, the more you appreciate other people. In addition, you will gain a greater awareness of the need to associate yourself with people who you can lift up and affirm you. You begin to recognize that you, too, have the power to be a positive influence in someone else's life.

As you move forward in life, take the time to truly think about who you are and the value you bring to this life. Then, look around you. Your relationships should reflect how you feel about yourself. When you feel good about you, others in relationship with you will do the same!

Always remember that no one can do you like you. So go ahead, step forward, and know that you can feel good about being "uniquely you!"

Reflections & Insights

Name 5 things you like about yourself. What characteristics set you apart from others?

_____

_____

_____

_____

_____

_____

_____

_____

_____

_____

_____

_____

_____

_____

_____

_____

_____

Find Your Reason to Live!

DAILY AFFIRMATION

"Today, I will seek to understand my purpose and my reason to live!"

EBB

It's amazing to me what can come out of a tough situation in life. We go through things that bring us to our knees. We endure situations we never dreamed we would have to face. Our hearts are constantly searching for a way to heal and be strengthened from the wounds that come with the trials, tribulations, and persecutions of life.

The struggles I endured as a single mom were nothing short of hard. So many times, I cried from the sheer exhaustion and emotional pain I felt in trying to do it all by myself. I rarely got a good night's sleep because I was constantly working and preparing myself for the next day's challenge. But, I was destined to work hard and stay in school so I could be a role model for my son. I was determined to be successful in life so that my sacrifice would not be in vain.

Making it through the hardships of single motherhood gave me an even stronger conviction to write my first book, SINGLE MOM, PHD. I knew if I could overcome the pain of a broken heart and broken relationships, my story could be used to help other single moms do the same. I wanted to offer them hope and remind them that they, too, could make it through the mental and emotional challenges of parenting alone. I wanted them to be encouraged to know that someone could identify with the hardships they were facing and be strengthened by the tools I used to overcome challenges in my life and relationships. In essence, I knew my story could be someone else's glory.

FLOW

I will forever be passionate about sharing the pain of my past. Because I have been broken myself, I know how important it is to offer hope and healing to those in need. I know how vital it is to remind those who are going through life's challenges, that there is a purpose for their pain. I know how critical it is to let people know that their struggle is not in vain, but can be used as a testimony to encourage those who are still going through the healing process.

Looking back over the course of my life, I now realize there was a reason I had to go through hard times and feel like there was no way out. There was a reason I had to experience the loneliness that came with no one really understanding the level of work that came with single motherhood. There was a reason I had to endure the pain of a broken heart and broken relationship.

131

I knew that, out of a very ugly situation, something beautiful could evolve. I knew someday I would be charged with telling my story so that others could be free and learn from the trials I faced in my life and relationships.

And it is for this reason that I have written, *Ebb & Flow*. I want to remind you that life will have its ups and downs and relationships will continue to ebb and flow. But through it all, you too can find the purpose for your pain and use your test to be a testimony to others who seek healing from a broken heart and broken relationships.

Most of all, you can find your reason to live. In writing this meditational guide, I found my reason to live...

That reason is *YOU*!

Reflections & Insights

Do you know what your purpose is on this Earth?
Name 3 ways you will seek to carry out that purpose in
your relationships.

_____

_____

_____

_____

_____

_____

_____

_____

_____

_____

_____

_____

_____

_____

_____

_____

_____

_____

My Prayer for You...

I am so humbled to have had this opportunity to spend the last 21 days with you. I pray that your life has been enriched and your heart renewed as you strive to build a heart-healthy life.

I pray you will continue on your journey with the understanding that there are so many things that are yet to be discovered. I pray you will always be reminded of who you are and the awesome ability you have to influence the lives of others for good. I pray that every barrier will be removed so that you can be anchored through the storms of life and allow love, forgiveness, and grace to heal your wounded soul.

I pray that *Ebb & Flow* will be used over and over again in your life to usher you to a healthy heart and healthy relationships.

This is my prayer for you...

I love you always and forever!

ABOUT THE AUTHOR

Tracey R. Brown, Ph.D.

Dr. Brown has been employed in the field of counseling and education for more than 23 years. She has served thousands of individuals and families helping them build a healthy life and healthy relationships.

Her personal life experiences as a single mom and professional career as a school counselor and administrator solidifies her passion to advocate for the human heart. Her message of hope offers encouragement to those who are downtrodden and in need of healing from the inside out.

Dr. Brown's mission is to help people realize their maximum potential and recognize the ability they have to positively affect the lives of others.

In addition to writing, Dr. Brown has also served as keynote speaker and seminar host in several states within the U.S. and abroad. She is also active in her local community and in various church organizations. She lives in Dallas, Texas, with her son, Zachary.

To contact Dr. Brown, visit her website at:
drtraceybrown.com

She can also be found on Facebook, Twitter, LinkedIn, and other social media sites